FIRST
ASSESSMENT PAPERS

REASONING

ANSWER BOOK

JM BOND

Nelson

Nelson Thornes Ltd
Delta Place
27 Bath Road
Cheltenham GL53 7TH
United Kingdom

© **J M Bond 1973, 1983, 1986, 1993**
First published by Thomas Nelson and Sons Ltd 1973
Second edition 1983
Revised edition 1986
Reprinted 1995

This fully revised edition 1993
Reprinted in 2001 by Nelson Thornes Ltd

Pupil's book	ISBN 0-17-424511-4
	NPN 12
Answer book	ISBN 0-17-424512-2
	NPN 01 02 03 04 05/10 9

By the same author
Introductory, First, Second, Third and Fourth Year
Assessment Papers in Mathematics

Introductory, First, Second, Third and Fourth Year
Assessment Papers in English

Second, Third and Fourth Year Assessment
Papers in Reasoning

Printed in Croatia by Zrinski d.d. Cakovec

There are two spaces in each line. Write in the missing numbers

1-2	2	4	6	8	10	12	14
3-4	27	24	21	18	15	12	9
5-6	70	75	80	85	90	95	100

7-11   A line has been drawn through the middle of each of the pictures below. If both sides of each drawing are the same, write **S**. If the sides are different, write **D**.

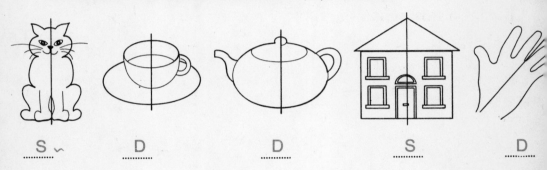

S   D   D   S   D

Take away one letter from the word on the left to leave another word.

Example: stare   We see it in the sky   star

12	read	Take away a letter to leave a colour.	re
13	vain	Take away a letter to leave a vehicle.	va
14	club	Take away a letter to leave a young lion.	cu
15	cast	Take away a letter to leave an animal.	ca
16	that	Take away a letter to leave something we wear.	ha

17 Which letter is found twice in **biscuit**? ....i....
18 Which letter is found three times in **sausages**? ....s....
19 How many times does **e** appear in **steerage**? ....3....
20 Which letter is found three times in **marmalade**? ....a....

Underline the correct word in the brackets.
21 All children have (coats, heads, hats)
22 All birds have (trees, berries, beaks)
23 All cats have (kittens, fur, milk)
24 All babies have (faces, bottles, prams)

Fill in the missing space on each line.

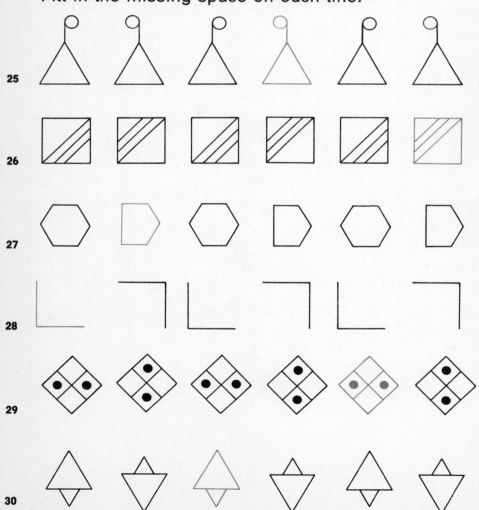

25

26

27

28

29

30

5

Paper 2

Underline the correct answer.

1. 41 is to 14 as 52 is to (41, 14, <u>25</u>, 52)
2. 6 is to 3 as 10 is to (8, <u>5</u>, 3, 6)
3. **ab** is to **ba** as **op** is to (<u>**po**</u>, **bo**, **pa**, **ap**)
4. 4 is to 8 as 6 is to (3, 8, 4, <u>12</u>)

Marks in a test were out of 20. Asif got 2 more than Danny. Bill lost 3 marks. Anna got full marks. Jane had 2 marks fewer than Bill. Danny got 8 marks fewer than Bill. Now fill in their names and marks.

		Name	Marks
5–6	First	Anna	20
7–8	Second	Bill	17
9–10	Third	Jane	15
11–12	Fourth	Asif	11
13–14	Fifth	Danny	9

15. If **rod** is written as 547, how would you write **odd**?   477
16. If **post** is 1234, how would you write **top**?   421
17. If **lamp** is 7056, how would **pal** be written?   607
18. If **star** is 4963, how would **rats** be written?   3694

Draw a line under the jumbled word and then write it correctly.

19–20. A <u>gip</u> lives in a sty.   pig

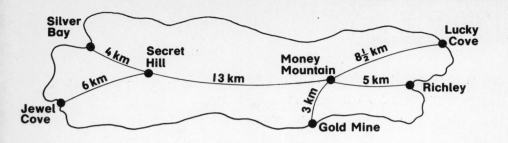

21 How far is it by road from Silver Bay to Money Mountain? _17 km_

22 How far is it from Jewel Cove to Money Mountain? _19 km_

23 How far is it from Gold Mine to Lucky Cove? _11½km_

24 How far is it from Secret Hill to Richley? _18 km_

25–27 Can you fit the following words into the square?
barn   twin   club

c	o	a	t
l			w
u			i
b	a	r	n

There were 110 pieces in a jigsaw. Anna guessed 81, Kim guessed 134 and Charlotte said 140.

8–30 _Kim_ was nearest, _Anna_ was second and _Charlotte_ third.

7

You can make six numbers from the figures 1, 2 and 3.
Write them in order, with the smallest first.

1 (1) 123   2 (2) 132

3 (3) 213   4 (4) 231

5 (5) 312   6 (6) 321

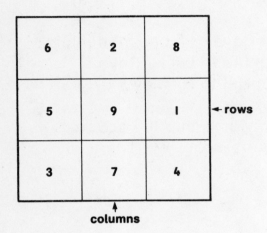

7 Add the numbers in the top row. 16

8 What is the total of the numbers in the middle row? 15

9 What is the sum of the numbers in the bottom row? 14

10 Add together the numbers in the left-hand column. 14

11 What is the sum of the numbers in the middle column? 18

12 What do the numbers in the right-hand column add up to? 13

Write the numbers of shapes which are the same.

13–14	<u>1 and 7</u>
15–16	<u>4 and 9</u>
17–18	<u>5 and 11</u>
19–20	<u>8 and 10</u>
21–24	Which drawings have no others the same as them? <u>2, 3, 6, 12</u>

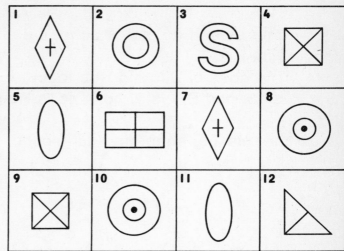

Here are the marks three children got in two tests.

	Maths	English
Alan	17	16
Rita	13	18
Cathy	15	15

25	Who got the same mark in both tests?	Cathy
26	Who scored over 15 in both tests?	Alan
27	Who got the lowest mark in either test?	Rita
28	Who got the highest mark in either test?	Rita
29	Who got the highest total marks?	Alan
30	Who got the lowest total marks?	Cathy

1 Jane is half as old as John. If John is 14, how old is Jane? _7_

2 The ages of Bill and Rob together equal that of Tom. If Tom is 16, and Bill is 9, how old is Rob? _7_

Draw the missing shape in each space.

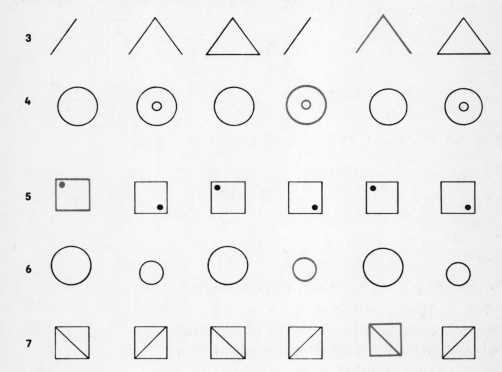

3

4

5

6

7

Draw a line under the jumbled word, and then write it correctly.

8 She broke her <u>nep</u> so she could not do her writing. per

9 "I do <u>ton</u> think I can go," said the boy. not

10 He was keen on cricket and liked to <u>tab</u>. ba

Draw a line under the two words which are made from the same letters.

1–12   <u>net</u>   pen   nip   <u>ten</u>   pan

3–14   pet   <u>tar</u>   rut   rot   <u>rat</u>

Underline any words below which have no two letters the same.

15–18   <u>aunt</u>   baby   niece   <u>uncle</u>   <u>lion</u>
sheep   <u>mouse</u>   stoat

These words follow a pattern. Write the word which should come next.

19	ran	run	ban	bun	fan	fun
20	no	not	go	got	do	dot
21	pat	pet	bat	bet	sat	set
22	cot	cut	pot	put	not	nut

Order these numbers and put a ring round the number (or amount) that is in the "middle" of the order.

23	8	11	12	6	(9)
24	(11)	8	13	10	12
25	£8.00	£11.00	£5.00	(£10.00)	£12.00
26	521	621	221	(421)	121

Sort out these jumbled sentences.

27   in kitchen mum the was.   Mum was in the kitchen.

28   went bus on the we.   We went on the bus.

29   do sums can your you?   Can you do your sums?

30   your where book is?   Where is your book?

Paper 5

Mark and Rajan like cricket. Ben and Carl like swimming.
Carl and Mark like rounders. Rajan and Ben like boxing.

1 Who likes swimming and boxing? ....Ben.....
2 Who likes cricket and rounders? ....Mark.....
3 Who likes boxing and cricket? ....Rajan.....
4 Who likes swimming and rounders? ....Carl.....

In each line there is one word which cannot be formed by using
the letters of the word on the left. Underline it.

5 **chips**   ship   hip   sip   <u>fish</u>
6 **snipe**   pen   <u>pea</u>   pin   sip
7 **heart**   the   rat   <u>rot</u>   tar
8 **parcel**   <u>lad</u>   lap   rap   cap

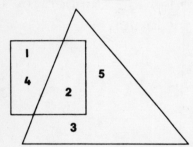

9 What is the sum of the numbers in the triangle? ....10.....
10 What is the sum of the numbers in the square? ....7.....
11 Which number is in both the square and the
triangle? ....2.....
12–13 Which numbers are in the square only? .....1 and 4.....
14–15 Which numbers are in the triangle only? .....3 and 5.....

12

16 If **old** is written as 642, which word is written as 2644?   <u>doll</u>

17 If **let** is written as 549, which word is 9455?   <u>tell</u>

18 If **tail** is written as 3216, which word is 613?   <u>lit</u>

19 If **taxi** is written as 1832, which word is 183?   <u>tax</u>

20 If **flat** is written as 2941, which word is 241?   <u>fat</u>

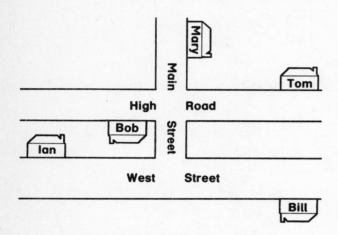

21 Bob lives in <u>High Road</u> 22 Ian lives in <u>West Street</u>

23 Bill lives in <u>West Street</u> 24 Mary lives in <u>Main Street</u>

25 Tom lives in <u>High Road</u>

26 Which of these words (litre, little, <u>litter</u>, listen) means rubbish?

27 Which of these words (<u>pitch</u>, pith, patch, pit) means a games field?

28 Which of these words (here, where, <u>away</u>, come) means absent?

29 Which of these words (<u>pleased</u>, please, glade) means glad?

30 Which of these words (<u>frown</u>, crown, gown) means scowl?

Paper 6

Some of the numbers in these sums have been left out. Can you fill them in?

1–2		3–4		5–6	
	1 4		3 4		2 5
	+ 3 5		+ 2 3		+ 2 1
	4 9		5 7		4 6

In each line two drawings are different from the others.
Underline them.

7–8

A847	A847	H847	A847	H847

9–10

Underline two words in each line which, though they are spelled differently, sound the same.

11–12 ball   tall   <u>bear</u>   tear   <u>bare</u>

13–14 told   <u>to</u>   do   <u>two</u>   tow

Look carefully at these sets of words and see how they are altered. Try to write in the missing word:

did → dud	pit → pot	can → cat
bid → bud	lit → lot	ban → bat
15 mid → <u>mud</u>	**16** hit → <u>hot</u>	**17** fan → <u>fat</u>

14

Underline the correct word in the brackets.

18 A cow gives us (milk, bacon, eggs)

19 A bee usually lives a (web, hive, shell)

20 A bird usually lives in a (byre, nest, cell)

21 All months have (May, years, days)

22 All games have (balls, players, bats)

23 A pig usually lives in a (tent, sty, nest)

24 200 + 10 + 8 = (302, 218, 290, 281, 812)

25 30 + 5 + 100 = (531, 900, 351, 135, 513)

6–30 Draw lines which will divide each shape into two equal parts.

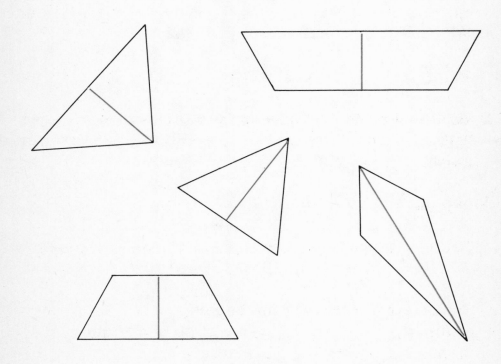

Paper 7

1 £1.00 is to 50p as 20p is to (<u>10p</u>, 5p, 50p, 100p)

2 **abc** is to **cba** as **xyz** is to (**xzy**, **xxz**, <u>**zyx**</u>, **zxy**)

Two words in each line are made up of the same letters. Underline them.

3–4 put <u>pat</u> tip top <u>tap</u>

5–6 out <u>act</u> cot cut <u>cat</u>

These words have been written in a number code, but they are jumbled up. Can you pair them correctly?

in	tin	it	inn
47	422	42	742

7–10 in __42__   tin __742__   it __47__   inn __422__

Underline the two words which are opposite in meaning.

11–12 <u>tall</u>   fat   <u>short</u>   small

13–14 away   <u>in</u>   gone   <u>out</u>

Fill in the gaps in each line.

15–16 2   22   3   33   _4_   44   _5_

17–18 77   _7_   66   6   55   5   _44_

19–20 2   4   _6_   8   10   12   _14_

21–24 Match each word with its meaning.

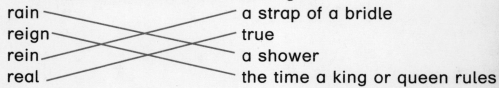

rain — a strap of a bridle
reign — true
rein — a shower
real — the time a king or queen rules

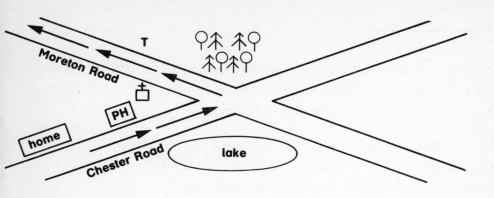

$\uparrow$ φ wood $\overset{+}{\Box}$ church   T telephone box   PH public house

25 As I walked along Chester Road, what did I pass on my left-hand side?   *a public house*

26 When I turned into Moreton Road, what was on my right-hand side?   *a wood*

27 What was on my left-hand side?   *a church*

28 As I was walking along Moreton Road, on which side of the road was the telephone box?   *right*

29 Underline the drawing which shows that two lots of eight make sixteen.

```
XXXX      XXXXXXXX      XXX        XXXXXXXXXXXXXXXX
XXXX      XXXXXXXX      XXXXX
XXXX                   XXX
                       XXXXX
```

30 Underline the drawing which shows that half of twelve is six.

```
XXXXXX    XXX    XXXX    XXXXXXXXXXXX
XXXXXX    XXX    XXXX
          XXX    XXXX
          XXX
```

Paper 8

From the list on the left-hand side of the page choose the words which best fill each space. Then, in the space, write the letter from the correct first half of the sentence.

1   There are 7   (a)   _b_ months in a year
2   There are 12   (b)   _d_ pence in the £1.00
3   There are 365   (c)   _f_ wheels on a bicycle
4   There are 100   (d)   _e_ toes on my right foot
5   There are 5   (e)   _c_ days in a year
6   There are 2   (f)   _a_ days in a week

Look at the these drawings carefully and answer the questions.

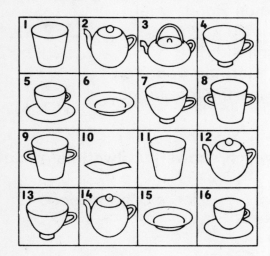

7–8   Which drawings are the same as No. 4?   7 and 13
9–10   Which drawings are the same as No. 14?   2 and 12
11   Which drawing is the same as No. 5?   16
12   Which drawing is the same as No. 1?   11
13   Which one is the same as No. 6?   15
14   Which one is the same as No. 8?   9
15–16   Which drawings have no others the same as them?   3 and 10

2   3   5   4   6

17   Add together the even numbers.   12

18   Add together the odd numbers.   8

19   Take the first number from the third number.   3

20   Take the number in the middle of the row from the last number.   1

21   Which of these is an animal? (Beer, dear, <u>deer</u>, dare)

22   Which of these is a fruit? (Pare, pair, pier, <u>pear</u>)

In each line there is one wrong number or amount. Underline it, and write the correct number at the end of the line.

23	5	10	15	20	25	<u>40</u>	30
24	36	33	<u>31</u>	27	24	21	30
25	70p	80p	90p	<u>£1.05</u>	£ 1.10	£ 1.20	£ 1.00

Draw in the missing shape in each line.

26

27

28

29

30   H   X   H   X   H   X

Paper 9

Take away the first and last letter of each word, and write the word which is left.

1 slates <u>late</u>   2 planet <u>lane</u>

3 flowers <u>lower</u>   4 chase <u>has</u>

In each line there is one word which cannot be formed by using the letters of the word on the left. Underline that word.

5 **poster**   stop   rope   <u>star</u>   post   rose   toe

6 **crates**   car   star   sea   race   <u>rot</u>   scar

7 **planet**   <u>tail</u>   ten   net   late   neat   pane

In each line two sums have the same answer. Underline the two sums.

8–9 $2 + 1$ $\underline{2 \times 2}$ 3×2 $\underline{4 \times 1}$ $2 + 2 + 3$

10–11 $\underline{3 + 7}$ $2 + 5$ 5×1 $\underline{10 \times 1}$ $10 + 1$

12–17   Put the words listed below into the order you would find them in a dictionary.

dog   cat   boy   duck   bat   comb

(1) <u>bat</u>   (2) <u>boy</u>   (3) <u>cat</u>

(4) <u>comb</u>   (5) <u>dog</u>   (6) <u>duck</u>

These words follow a pattern. Write the word which should come next.

18 pit   tip   loop   pool   evil   <u>live</u>

19 red   read   led   lead   bed   <u>bead</u>

20 fan   flan   can   clan   pan   <u>plan</u>

21 pop   poop   hop   hoop   lop   <u>loop</u>

20

Look at this diagram:

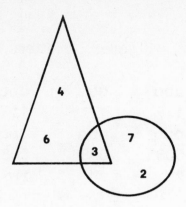

22	What is the sum of all the numbers in the triangle?	13
23	What is the sum of all the numbers in the circle?	12
24	Which number is in both the triangle and the circle?	3
25	What is the sum of the numbers in the circle only?	9
26	What is the sum of the numbers in the triangle only?	10

Underline the correct answer in the brackets.

27 A book always has (sums, pictures, pages).

28 A bird's egg always has (a cup, a shell, a spoon).

29 A calendar always has (dates, minutes, pictures).

30 Rain is always (cold, wet, heavy).

In each line one group of figures or letters is different from the others. Underline it.

1	aba	<u>aab</u>	aba	aba	aba
2	117	117	117	<u>171</u>	117
3	qpq	qpq	<u>opq</u>	qpq	qpq
4	<u>080</u>	008	008	008	008
5	zff	zff	zff	zff	<u>zfz</u>

There is a space in each line. Fill in the missing letter or number

6	6	7	8	<u>9</u>	10	11	12
7	33	32	31	30	<u>29</u>	28	27
8	50	<u>60</u>	70	80	90	100	110
9	6	16	7	17	8	18	<u>9</u>
10	a9	b8	<u>c7</u>	d6	e5	f4	g3

Underline any words which begin and end with the same letter.

11–12	<u>comic</u>	pasta	<u>level</u>	step	rare
13–14	boots	<u>shoes</u>	bold	code	<u>else</u>
14–16	<u>edge</u>	deer	start	<u>treat</u>	each

Write **true** or **false** against each of these sentences.

17 All girls have fair hair. <u>false</u>

18 Girls never have dark hair. <u>false</u>

19 Some boys are fair and some are dark. <u>true</u>

Look at this map:

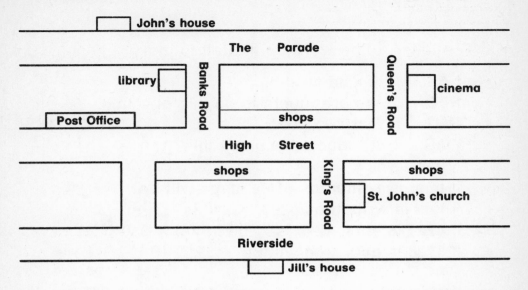

20 On which road is the cinema?   Queen's Road
21 On which road is the Post Office?   High Street
22 On which road is St. John's Church?   King's Road
23 On which road is the library?   Banks Road

24–27 If Jill went to the cinema using the   Riverside
       quickest way, on which roads and streets   King's Road
       would she have to walk?   High Street
                                                                      Queen's Road

28–30 The divisor is the number by which you divide.
       Fill in the missing divisors in the following sums.

$$2\overline{)\,24} = 12 \qquad 3\overline{)\,18} = 6 \qquad 4\overline{)\,16} = 4$$

Paper 11

Add one letter to the word on the left to make another word.

1	**LAP**	A kind of light	LAMP
2	**RED**	We are taught to do this at school	READ
3	**HAD**	Part of your body	HAND (or HEAD)
4	**FOG**	A tadpole becomes this	FROG

5 If **post** is written as 6145, **stops** will be   45164

6 If **fast** is written as 4293, 93244 is   staff

7 If 4221 is **soot**, 1244 is   toss

8 If 1728 is **near**, **ran** will be   821

9 If May 1st is a Thursday, what day was April 30th?   Wednesday

10 Which letter occurs twice in **autumn**?   u

11 Which letter is found twice in **cricket**?   c

12 What letter is in rook but not in **robin**?   k

Can you fill in the figures which have been left out of these sums?

13–14	15–16	17–18
4 3	5 4	6 5
− 3 1	− 2 1	− 2 1
1 2	3 3	4 4

19–21 Draw a line under each word which contains the letters **a**, **b** and **c**.

abandon   accent   <u>bacon</u>   accident   <u>cabin</u>   about   <u>cabbage</u>

Draw the missing shape in each space.

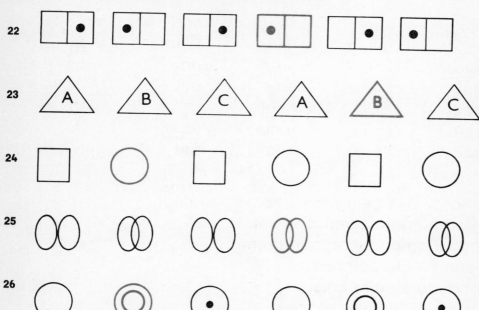

22

23

24

25

26

Underline the two words on each line which are formed from the same letters.

27–28   eat   <u>den</u>   dad   and   <u>end</u>

29–30   <u>ten</u>   <u>net</u>   not   tin   tan

Underline two words in each line which, though they are spelled differently, sound the same.

1–2	sand	<u>sun</u>	send	<u>son</u>	sin
3–4	seat	meant	<u>meat</u>	team	<u>meet</u>
5–6	<u>knew</u>	knot	men	<u>new</u>	know
7–8	boy	<u>buy</u>	day	bay	<u>by</u>
9–10	<u>heel</u>	win	<u>heal</u>	in	men
11–12	safe	sail	male	<u>sale</u>	salt
13–14	saw	set	<u>sea</u>	me	<u>see</u>

Four children are going to do some painting.
Alison and Mark use yellow paint.
David and Emma use orange paint.
Alison and Emma paint dogs.
David and Mark paint cats.

15 Who paints yellow dogs? Alison
16 Who paints orange cats? David
17 Who paints orange dogs? Emma
18 Who paints yellow cats? Mark

Underline the correct word in the brackets.
19 Mew is to cat as bark is to (tree, sheep, <u>dog</u>)
20 Water is to drink as bread is to (<u>eat</u>, plate, cup)
21 Cuckoo is to bird as poodle is to (bull, farm, <u>dog</u>)
22 July is to June as May is to (June, <u>April</u>, March)
23 5p is to 10p as 50p is to (5p, 10p, <u>£1.00</u>)

24 A "good home" is (a large house, a house with a large garden, <u>somewhere the cat will be looked after</u>)

25 If you would like one of these kittens, what should you do first? (Write a letter, <u>telephone</u>, go to see them)

26 You are asked to telephone
(<u>during the day</u>, night time only, in the evening)

27–30 Can you put the words below in the right places in the square?
ends   blue   boat   ties

b	o	a	t
l	■	■	i
u	■	■	e
e	n	d	s

Paper 13

Two drawings in each line are the same. Underline them.

1–2

3–4

Thirty days hath September,
April, June, and November.
All the rest have thirty-one,
Except February alone
Which hath but twenty-eight days clear
And twenty-nine in each leap year.

Write the number of days in each month for the year 1996.

	January	31			
5	February	29	11	August	31
6	March	31	12	September	30
7	April	30	13	October	31
8	May	31	14	November	30
9	June	30	15	December	31
10	July	31			

Sort out these jumbled sentences.

16 towel where the is? Where is the towel?

17 pence costs it ten. It costs ten pence.

18 your library change book. Change your library book.

19 dirty wash hands your. Wash your dirty hands.

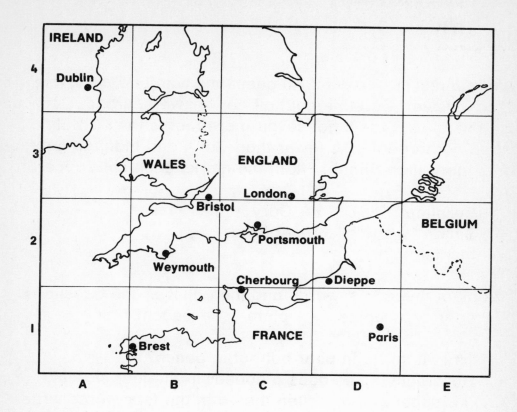

To help us to find places, some maps are divided into squares. The columns are given letters and the rows are numbered. Which squares are these towns in? (Put the letter before the number.)

20	London	C3	21	Weymouth	B2
22	Paris	D1	23	Brest	B1
24	Dublin	A4	25	Cherbourg	C1
26	Bristol	B3	27	Dieppe	D2
28	Portsmouth	C2			

Sort out these jumbled words to make the names of two fruits.

29 aaabnn   banana

30 leppa   apple

Paper 14

We had a test. There were 40 questions with one mark for each correct answer. Caroline got half her answers wrong. Gary made eight mistakes. Simon got seven more marks than Caroline. Andrea got three marks fewer than Gary, and Manjula got four marks more than Simon. Fill in the marks each child received.

1 Caroline _20_   2 Gary _32_
3 Simon _27_   4 Andrea _29_
5 Manjula _31_

Look at these four words and then answer the questions.
pear   apple   plum   peach

6 What letter is in **pear** but not in **peach**? _r_
7 How many times does **p** appear in the four words? _5_
8 If **e** appears more often than **a** in the four words write X. If they appear the same number of times write Y. _Y_
9 Which of the words does not contain the letter **e**? _plum_

Underline the smallest number, and ring the largest.

10–11	45	43	(54)	34	44
12–13	312	123	231	213	(321)
14–15	(541)	415	145	451	154

One number or letter in each line is wrong. Underline it, and write the correct number at the end of the line.

16–17	3	6	9	13	15	12
18–19	45	40	53	30	25	35
20–21	d	e	f	g	i	h

30

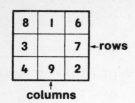

8	1	6
3		7	←rows
4	9	2

↑
columns

22 What number must I put in the middle of the square so that all the rows add up to the same number? 5

23 What number does each row add up to? 15

24 What number is in the middle of the top row? 1

25 What number is at the left-hand side of the bottom row? 4

January   Spring starts on 21st March
February   Summer starts on 21st June
March   Autumn starts on 23rd September
April   Winter starts on 21st December
May
June
July
August
September
October
November
December

In which seasons are these months?

26 May   spring   29 August summer

27 January   winter   30 February winter

28 October   autumn

Paper 15

One sum in each line has a different answer from the others.
Underline it.

1 4×2 $\underline{5 + 4}$ $3 + 5$ $9 - 1$
2 6×1 3×2 $\underline{3 + 2}$ 2×3
3 $\underline{4 \times 0}$ $5 - 1$ 2×2 $3 + 1$
4 3×3 $12 - 3$ $8 + 1$ $\underline{5 \times 2}$
5 $3 + 4$ $8 - 1$ $\underline{4 + 2}$ $6 + 1$

Are the following statements true or false? Write T for true and F
for false.

6   There are 100 ml in a litre.   _F_
7   There are 100 pence in £1.00.   _T_
8   There are 12 months in a year.   _T_
9   Twenty 20 pence pieces make £2.00.   _F_
10 1 000 metres make one km.   _T_

11 sting   Take away a letter and leave something we can
all do.   _sing_

12 trail   Take away a letter and leave part of an
animal.   _tail_

13 haunt   Take away a letter and leave a relation.
aunt

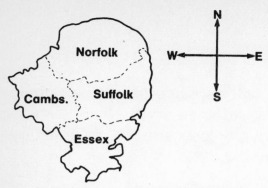

14	Which county is north of Suffolk?	Norfolk
15	Which county is south of Suffolk?	Essex
16	Which county is west of Suffolk?	Cambs
17	Which county is south of Norfolk?	Suffolk

Underline any word in which no letters are the same.

18–21 eager   <u>trail</u>   boots   <u>mango</u>   spots   <u>scent</u>

sales   start   peace   <u>worse</u>   free   edge

In each line there is a space. Draw in the missing shape.

22

23

24

Two words in each line are formed from the same letters.
Underline them.

25–26 <u>ate</u>   tar   <u>tea</u>   ale   are

27–28 nab   <u>bin</u>   bun   not   <u>nib</u>

29–30 <u>two</u>   too   <u>tow</u>   wet   ten

33

Paper 16

1   In three years' time Henry will be twice as old as I am now. If I am eight now, how old is Henry? _13_

2   If I had 3p more I would have twice as much as my sister who has 9p. How much have I? _15p_

In each line two drawings are the same. Underline them.

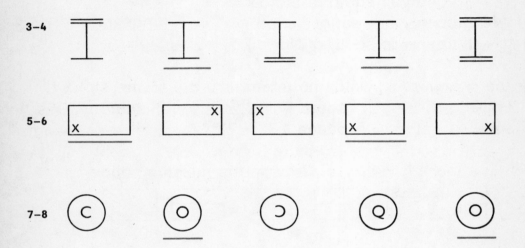

3–4

5–6

7–8

Underline the correct word in the brackets.

9   Ship is to water as plane is to (engine, air, crew)

10   Come is to go as down is to (fall, up, slide)

11   Cod is to fish as beef is to (meat, cow, bacon)

12   House is to people as stable is to (sty, men, horses)

13   Sea is to swim as land is to (air, walk, water)

In each space write the missing numbers or letters.

14	ab	ba	_ab_	ba	ab	ba
15	246	642	246	_642_	246	642
16	a2	b3	a2	b3	_a2_	b3

34

There are two spaces in each line. Fill in the correct numbers.

17–18   28   24   _20_   16   12   _8_   4
19–20   3   _6_   9   _12_   15   18   21

Here are the distances of some towns from London.

Manchester   296 km   Warwick   144 km
Norwich   184 km   Swansea   320 km

21 The nearest town to London is   _Warwick_
22 The second nearest is   _Norwich_
23 The third nearest is   _Manchester_
24 The fourth nearest is   _Swansea_

25 If I dropped my purse somewhere in the town I should report it to (the bank, the Post Office, <u>the police</u>, the bus station)
26 Rearrange the letters **abc** to form a word.   _cab_

Before you start cooking

   1 Read the recipe.
   2 Put on an apron or overall.
   3 Wash your hands.
   4 Collect all the utensils you need.
   5 Always use an oven glove when handling hot utensils.

27 What should you do to stop your hands getting burned? (Wash them, <u>use an oven glove</u>, use an overall)
28 How can you stop your clothes getting dirty? (<u>Wear an apron</u>, wash them, clear away afterwards)
29 A recipe is (a record, <u>instructions for cooking something</u>, a story book)
30 You should wash your hands (because they are dirty, to warm them, <u>because you don't want any germs to get in the food</u>, to keep the apron clean)

Paper 17

1 (Pits, snap, <u>snip</u>) is **pins** spelled backwards.
2 (<u>Drab</u>, drip, brad) is **bard** spelled backwards.
3 (Post, <u>spot</u>, stop) is **tops** spelled backwards.
4 (Fowl, bowl, <u>flow</u>) is **wolf** spelled backwards.
5 (<u>Evil</u>, vile, veil) is **live** spelled backwards.
6 (<u>Pots</u>, post, soup) is **stop** spelled backwards.

7–14 Fill in the missing numbers.

1 1	1 2	2 4	2 3
× 4	× 3	× 2	× 3
4 4	3 6	4 8	6 9

I expect you have seen stained glass windows in churches. You can pick out St. David because he always holds a leek. St. Matthew has a bible and a purse, and St. Crispin has his cobbler's tools.

15 (<u>St. David</u>, St. Matthew, St. Crispin) has a vegetable.
16 (St. David, <u>St. Matthew</u>, St. Crispin) holds the money.
17 Who do you think is the patron saint of shoemakers? (St. David, St. Matthew, <u>St. Crispin</u>)
18 St. David is the patron saint of Wales. What do you think the Welsh emblem is? (A shoe, <u>a leek</u>, a purse)
19 Who do you think was a tax collector? (St. David, <u>St. Matthew</u>, St. Crispin)

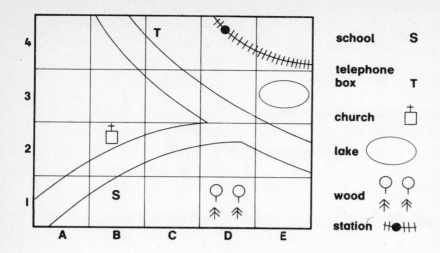

school	S
telephone box	T
church	†
lake	(oval)
wood	(wood symbol)
station	(station symbol)

20 The telephone box is in square   <u>C4</u>
21 The lake is in square   <u>E3</u>
22 The church is in square   <u>B2</u>
23 The wood is in square   <u>D1</u>
24 The station is in square   <u>D4</u>
25 The school is in square   <u>B1</u>

26 Guy Fawkes tried to blow up Parliament in 1605. What was the date five years after this? (1650, 1655, <u>1610</u>, 1615)

27 Columbus discovered America in 1492. What was the date ten years after this? (<u>1502</u>, 1493, 1592, 1493)

28 The Battle of Hastings was in 1066. What was the date ten years earlier? (966, 1065, 1055, <u>1056</u>)

29 Underline the drawing which shows that 3 lots of 6 = 18.

```
XXXXXXXXX    XXXX    XXX    XXXXX
XXXXXXXXX    XXXX    XXX    XXXXX
             XXXX    XXX    XXXXX
             XXXX    XXX    XXXXX
                     XXX
                     XXX
```
<u>(third column underlined)</u>

30 Which of these numbers can be made by multiplying a number by itself? (48, <u>36</u>, 30, 34, 18)

Sort out these jumbled words.
They are all the names of items of clothing.

1–7	vets	telb	janes	sightt	trish	tha	ocks
	vest	belt	jeans	tights	shirt	hat	sock

Underline the drawing in the brackets which would be next in the series.

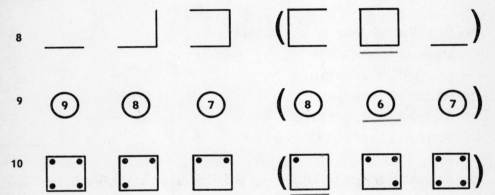

8

9

10

11 Which letter is found twice in **sparrow** and once in **robin**?
...r...

12 Which letter is in **spade** and also in **dig**?
...d...

13 Which letter comes three times in **themselves**?
...e...

14 Which letter is in **den** and also in **lion**?
...n...

15 Which letter is found three times in **excellent**?
...e...

16 Which letter is found three times in **banana** and once in **apple**?
...a...

Key

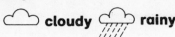 cloudy   rainy

 sunny   snow

thundery

17	In the north it was	raining
18	In the south it was	sunny
19	In the west it was	cloudy
20	In the east it was	thundery

Here are four words, and underneath them are four sets of numbers. They are not under the right words. Can you find out which numbers belong to which words?

too	out	tot	to
247	727	72	722

21 **too** should be   722   22 **out** should be   247

23 **tot** should be   727   24 **to** should be   72

Underline the correct answer in the brackets.

25 3 is to 6 as 6 is to (3, 12, 6)

26 £1.00 is to 50p as 10p is to (£1.00, 50p, 5p)

27 10 is to 100 as 50 is to (500, 50, 5)

28 16 is to 8 as 18 is to (6, 8, 9)

29 20 is to 10 as 24 is to (42, 12, 14)

30 5 is to 15 as 7 is to (35, 28, 21)

Paper 19

DECEMBER						
Sun	Mon	Tues	Wed	Thur	Fri	Sat
		1	2	3	4	5
6	7	8	9	10	11	12
13	14	15	16	17	18	19
20	21	22	23	24	25	26
27	28	29	30	31		

1 How many days are there in this month? _31_

2 Christmas Day is on a Friday

3 A fortnight after Wednesday,
   December 2nd is December 16th

4 What day is the first day of the month? Tuesday

5-7 Which days occur five times in
     this month? Tuesday,
                  Wednesday
                  and Thursday

8 What day will January 1st be? Friday

9 What is the date of the third Monday in
   the month? December 21st

Put the following words in alphabetical order:

dog   cat   donkey   cow   bull

10 (1) ...... bull ......   11 (2) ...... cat ......   12 (3) ...... cow ......

13 (4) ...... dog ......   14 (5) ...... donkey ......

Take one letter away from the word on the left to leave another word.

15 break   Take away a letter to leave part of a bird.   beak

16 black   Take away a letter to leave the opposite of
           front.   back

17 fowl   Take away a letter to leave a bird.   owl

18 least   Take away a letter to leave the opposite of
           first.   last

In each space write the missing numbers or letters.

19	531	135	531	135	531	135
20	23	34	45	23	34	45
21	5 × 6	6 × 5	5 × 6	6 × 5	5 × 6	6 × 5
22	2 × 5	2 × 6	2 × 7	2 × 8	2 × 9	2 × 10
23	a5	b6	c7	a5	b6	c7

Are the following statements right or wrong? At the end of each line write **R** if it is right, or **W** if it is wrong.

24 There are always seven days in a week.   R

25 It is always wet on Wednesdays.   W

26 August comes before July.   W

27 All flowers are yellow.   W

28 An elephant is a large animal.   R

29 Your elbow is part of your leg.   W

30 Some cars are green.   R

We played a cricket match. If Paul had scored 6 more he would have got 20 runs. Sharon got 2 more than Paul. Sally scored half as many as Paul. If Darren had scored one more he would have got the same as Sharon. If Tim had scored 3 more he would have got half as many as Sharon.

1-5 Fill in their scores.

Paul _14_ Sharon _16_ Sally _7_ Darren _15_ Tim _5_

Mrs. Brown's house has three windows upstairs, two windows downstairs and two chimneys. Mr. Ford's house has four windows upstairs, two windows downstairs and two chimneys. Mr. Todd's house has two windows upstairs, two windows downstairs and two chimneys. The Deans' house has two windows upstairs, two windows downstairs and three chimneys. Miss White's house has three windows upstairs, one window downstairs and three chimneys. Put the right name under each house.

6-10 Miss White   Mr. Ford   Mr. Todd   Mrs. Brown   The Deans

Underline the sum on each line which has a different answer from the others.

11	$2 + 1$	3×1	$4 - 1$	$\underline{2 + 2}$
12	2×3	$\underline{5 - 1}$	$5 + 1$	$7 - 1$
13	3×3	$10 - 1$	$\underline{8 - 1}$	$8 + 1$

How many different letters are there in each of the following words?

14 banana 3   15 coffee 4   16 engine 4

17 hollow 4   18 cocoa 3   19 terrier 4

In each space write the missing numbers or letters.

20	1d2	2d1	1d2	2d1	1d2	2d1
21	axa	bxb	axa	bxb	axa	bxb
22	a1	b2	c3	d4	e5	f6

Underline the drawing in the brackets which would be the next in the series.

23 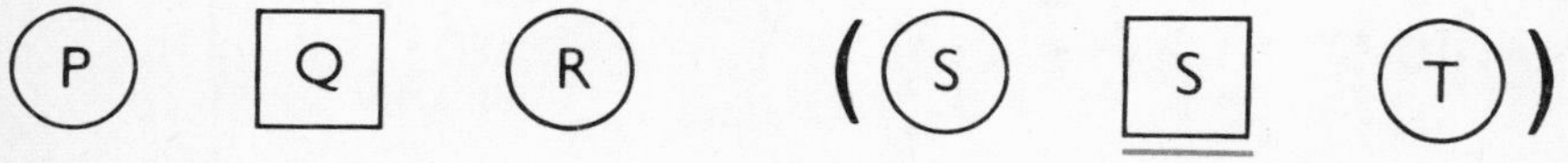

24 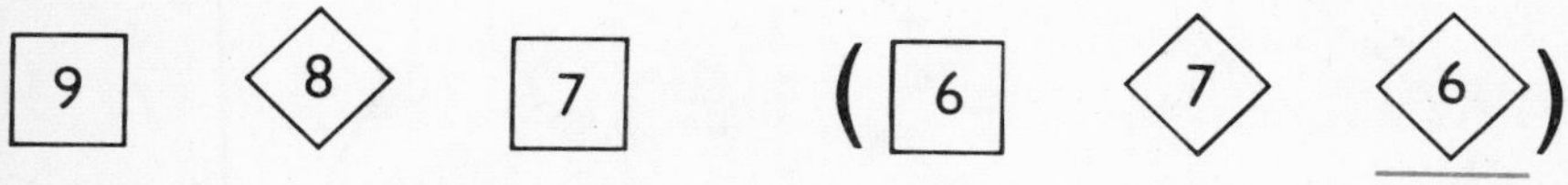

25 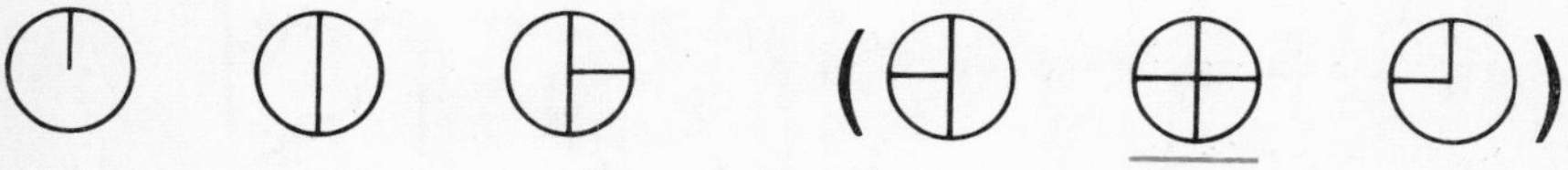

26 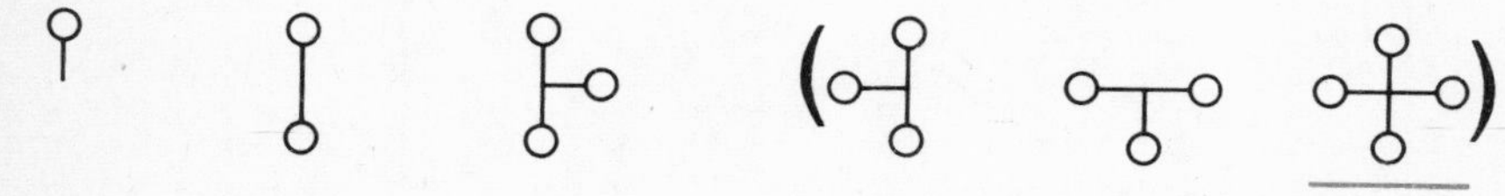

Can you fit these words into this square?

27–30 said soft date tale

s	a	i	d
o			a
f			t
t	a	l	e

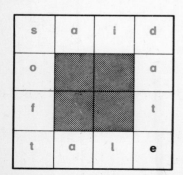

Underline the numbers or letters in the brackets which would be next in the series.

1	ab	ac	ad	(<u>ae</u>	af	be)
2	24	35	46	(64	56	<u>57</u>)
3	98	87	76	(54	<u>65</u>	66)
4	b2	c3	d4	(f5	e6	<u>e5</u>)

A line has been drawn through the middle of each of the shapes below.
If both sides of each shape are the same write **S**. If the sides are different write **D**.

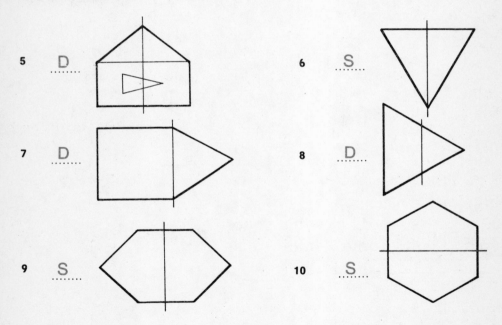

5 D

6 S

7 D

8 D

9 S

10 S

These words follow a pattern. Write the word which should come next.

11	wan	wane	ban	bane	man	mane
12	man	men	fan	fen	pan	pen
13	bell	ball	cell	call	tell	tall

There are two spaces in each line. Write in the missing numbers.

14–15	41	_39_	37	35	33	31	_29_
16–17	2	7	12	_17_	22	27	_32_
18–19	_2_	12	3	13	4	_14_	5

Underline the correct answer in the brackets.

20   2 is to 20 as 4 is to (24, 30, <u>40</u>, 20)

21   100 is to 10 as 300 is to (3, 20, 300, <u>30</u>)

22   D is to letter as 7 is to (days, month, <u>number</u>)

Here is a part of a train timetable:

Appleby	Barnston		Denton
depart	arrive	depart	arrive
08.30	08.40	08.45	09.30

23   How long does the train stop at Barnston?
(1 min, <u>5 min,</u> 10 min, 30 min)

24   How long does it take to travel from Appleby to Barnston?
(5 min, 30 min, 20 min, <u>10 min</u>)

25   How long does it take to go from Barnston to Denton?
(5 min, 10 min, <u>45 min,</u> 30 min)

26   How long does it take to travel from Appleby to Denton?
(<u>60 min,</u> 30 min, 45 min)

In each line the letters of one word have been jumbled up. Draw a line under that word, and write it correctly at the end of the line.

27   Tim cut his finger and it was very <u>rose</u>.   sore

28   <u>Tans</u> are little insects.   ants

29   "Hurry up," said Dad. "You're too <u>owls</u>."   slow

30   Little Red Riding Hood met the <u>flow</u>.   wolf

Paper 22

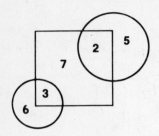

1   What number is in the square only? ___7___

2   What number is in the small circle only? ___6___

3   What number is in the large circle only? ___5___

4   What is the total of the numbers in the square? ___12___

5   What is the total of the numbers in the small circle? ___9___

6   What is the total of the numbers in the square only? ___7___

7   What is the total of all the numbers? ___23___

8   What number is in the large circle and also in the square? ___2___

9   What number is in the small circle and also in the square? ___3___

Draw in the missing shape in each line.

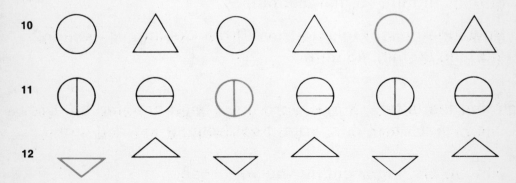

46

Underline two words in each line which, though they are spelled differently, sound the same.

13–14	blue	bawl	bad	blew	bow
15–16	there	hear	hoard	hard	here
17–18	rose	rude	rows	rays	rain
19–20	tier	their	where	there	here

The chart below shows how many comics were sold at a shop last week.

Monday	Tuesday	Wednesday	Thursday	Friday	Saturday
27	36	19	40	39	57

21 On which day were fewest sold? Wednesday

22 On which day were most sold? Saturday

23 How many more were sold on Saturday than on Thursday? 17

24 How many fewer were sold on Tuesday than on Friday? 3

25 How many more were sold on Saturday than on Monday? 30

Sort out these jumbled sentences.

26 dishes the washed he. He washed the dishes.

27 her read she book. She read her book.

28 boots clean your football. Clean your football boots.

29 up went hill Jill the. Jill went up the hill.

30 very early arrived she. She arrived very early.

47

DATE

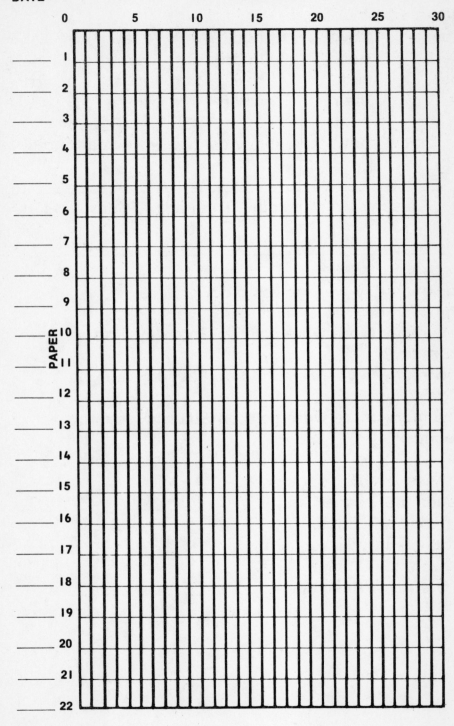

TOTAL MARKS

PAPER